Stop, Rest, and Think

(Volumes I - III: An eclectic collection of reflections, musings, passages, essays, short story fiction and other material.)

by Fuad A. Kamal

This book is intended to provide accurate information with regard to the subject matter covered. However, any work may contain errors. No responsibility is accepted by the publisher or author for inaccuracies, omissions, or typographical or other errors. The author and publisher specifically disclaim any loss, risk, or liability, whether personal, legal, financial, or otherwise, direct or indirect, incurred under any theory of liability, as a consequence, from the use and/or application of any of this book's contents. Testimonials reflect views and submissions at the time we receive them. Individual testimonials do not necessarily imply endorsement by the institutions or entities associated with the individuals.

This work includes works of fiction. Incidents, names, characters and places are fictitious or used fictitiously. Any resemblance to actual persons, living or dead, or events is coincidental.

Library of Congress Control Number: 2009905999
ISBN: 978-1-59236-003-1
Publisher: Desert Well Network LLC
www.desertwellnetwork.com
Book Website:
www.StopRestAndThink.com

v .9

Table of Contents

Note to Readers

Please note that Vol I , II or III may appeal to different audiences. Vol I is short items, Vol II includes essays and other material. Vol III is short story fiction,

Flip to whichever section you are interested in first.

(Works of fiction include The Man, the Mosquito and the Hut, A Most Unnatural Day, On Writing a Story, A Mother's Love, Time Court, Democracy to Dictatorship 2.0.)

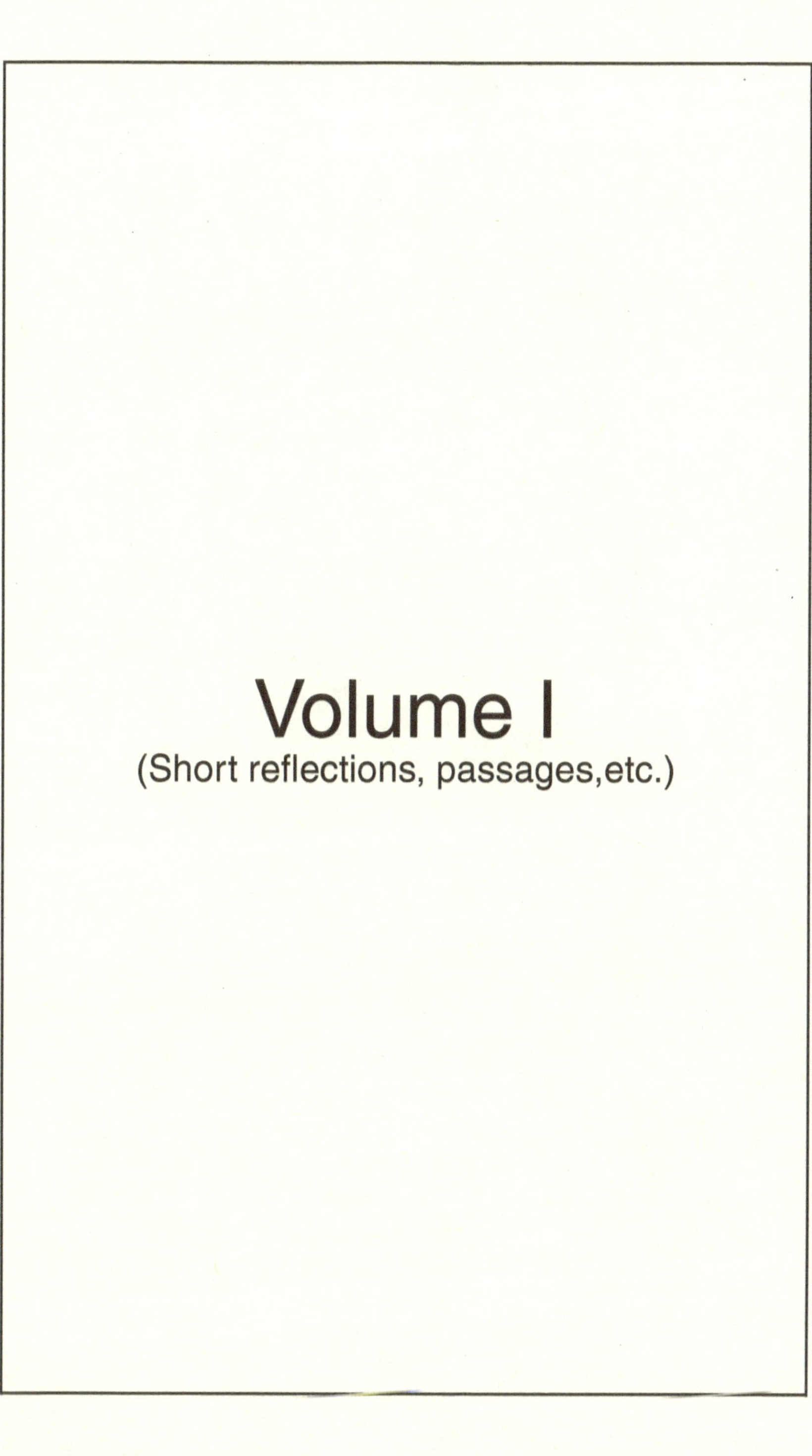

Volume I

(Short reflections, passages,etc.)

Surely a smile
needs no
translation?

Works anywhere
in the world!

Know what is important. Persevere. If one is dealt thorns in life, look for roses. Where there are thorns, surely roses cannot be hidden too far behind? Is not a rose is flanked by thorns? Is not a sunset followed by a sunrise?

Don't despair.
Sometimes the
fastest road
to success
runs through
failure.

One has considerable control
over one's actions.

Limited (if any) control over
someone else's reaction to one's
original action.

Considerable control over one's
reaction, to someone else's
reaction, to one's initial action.

One has an advantage in
life if one can understand
what one has more (or less)
control of (and can act on that
information.)

If you lost everything today, how would you value every loss? Know your values. Nothing simplifies life more quickly.

Life without
hope is like food
without salt. Life
without love
is like a world
without color.

In life, one of the
most difficult
debts to fully repay
is that of a child to
a good mother.

Thank your
mother today!

If love is a
garden, laughter
are the flowers
that grow in it.

Justice is security
- just as injustice
invites instability.
Truth is strength. And
compassion is beauty.

So build your home
in life on a secure
foundation of justice,
with the sturdy walls
of truth surrounded by
the beautiful gardens of
compassion.

It is amazing how much can be accomplished with honesty and a little bit of hard work.

Small actions done continuously over a long period of time will usually defeat a single, dramatic action done only once.

Perhaps not unlike two people who go to the gym. One is wildly enthusiastic on the first day and spends hours working out, but then never returns to the gym again. Compare this to the other one who approaches the workouts in a disciplined way. The first day's workout may just a be few minutes, but the person continues the workouts a few minutes every day for the rest of his or her life. Who do you think will benefit more from the gym?

Try to find someone worthless - someone without any gifts.

One mind-set is that you never will. If one is not arrogant, one may be able to tap value from seemingly unlikely situations.

Sometimes, failure (or fear of it) forces one to learn how things work far beyond one would have thought possible (or necessary.)

The fruit of such an experience, in hindsight, may reveal a disguised gift –a skill toolset for the rest of your life.

Conversely, sometimes easy success can hide complacency and ignorance.

The ease of building on one's strengths can lull one into overlooking the inconvenience of one's weaknesses. This can rob one of the relationships necessary to mitigate one's weaknesses. The loss of such relationships makes the world a poorer place. Giving one's weaknesses voice is seldom gratifying, but building human connections to make oneself better, makes us all richer.

Fear is a thief, that robs
one's better instincts.
Arrogance makes one
blind.

A civilization feeding
on both is inevitably
in an undiscovered
war with itself.

Unconditional charity
and sacrifice combined
with unbridled passion
and without expectation
of material return, seeds
a well so deep that it
is one of the very few
things that can, in time,
transform a hopelessly
barren desert into an
flourishing vibrant oasis.

If you want to know
if you are on the right
path, see who chooses to
befriend you.

Unfortunately,
whenever one is doing
something really
important, some people
will always dislike you.

Just make sure that
the right people
like/dislike you.

Nothing increases intelligence like a little humility does.

(Try it with your spouse if you don't believe me.)

Personal attacks are a type of destructive, negative criticism.

Instead, if one needs to criticize do it positively.

Engage in constructive problem-solving, ideally with a dash of genuine empathy.

As an added bonus, throw in a genuine compliment, if you can. (Surely, that person is not doing *everything* wrong?)

It's amazing just
how many people
in society don't
want to think,
and would gladly
abdicate that
function to others.

It's truly telling
how much more
intelligent another
person becomes
in one's estimation
— if one is willing
to see things
through that other
person's eyes.

Few things
would cure as
much of the
world's ills as
a large dose
of empathy.

Increasingly, science fiction seems to be smashing into science. Some of today's truths may be tomorrow's rejected ideas, and among today's outlandish notions may be tomorrow's truths. Knowledge seems to have no end in sight as it is likely to churn through dizzying paradigm shifts.

Many things in life
are self-fulfilling
prophesies —
particularly if people
really believe in them.
But do we, as a people,
have the courage to
dream the big dreams?
Unfortunately,
too often not. But
just imagine if we
did? What could
we not accomplish
when dreams are
seeded into reality?

Are all people and
experiences the same?
Too often, people
allocate time, money and
effort uniformly in their
life. Wisdom is knowing
those particularly unique
moments in one's life
when to sharply change
those unquestioned
allocations. Not
capriciously, but with
deep insight into oneself.

Among the most
bitter fruit of time
is *regret*.

Among the most
careless, in the
harvest they sow,
are the arrogant.

Man is amassing
mind-boggling
power while
hurtling into a
headlong collision
with complexity.
Press "Upgrade" or
it's "Game Over".

Today the
average person
in a developed
economy lives
better than
the wealthiest
entrepreneurs and
kings of only a few
hundred years ago.

Will tomorrow's
eight year old
be studying
macroeconomics,
calculus and
general relativity?

One day I randomly flashed on an old memory. I remembered being at a team-building training camp. I also recalled how an individual had encouraged and motivated someone else through a difficult task. He had told her to break up the task - to do it one step at a time. When she was confronted with a simpler step, rather than the difficult task, she was able to apply herself to the task. The task than just collapsed into a sequence of simpler steps.

Break down an impossible task into parts. Then it just might read i m possible.

If you want your soul to shout with joy— give, give, and give.

The laughter
of children
reminds one
of the music
in one's soul.

Life Equations

What costs (in terms of time, money, effort, sacrifice, hardship, etc.) have you voluntarily and conscientiously taken upon yourself to reflect the actual values of different dimensions of your character?

If you see a good person following their heart, support them if even with just a word. If enough people did it, the world would be transformed.

There are two types of power. One is like a rock. Another is like water. In time, water wears away the rock.

Love may be soft, the night may be sharp. But don't forget to love patiently, even when the night is dark and very long.

Do you want to know
of a good bargain?
Invest in your heart.
Feed it. Use your heart
to see the best. Use
your heart to hear the
best. Zealously guard
it from darkness.
Grow a light in your
heart and thereby
find peace in yourself.

Life has a beat.
Align the base
rhythm to
your heartbeat.
Make your
soul dance.

There is a popular board game called "chutes and ladders". [1] In the game of life, perhaps one can contemplate good people as ladders and bad ones as chutes. See where you are in life, and then examine the people in your life..

[1] The game "snakes and ladders" might be the better analogy in some nations.

Don't despair.
Listen to factual
criticism,
especially if it is
from a competitor.
Oops ... looks like
they just told you
precisely how to
beat them.

Success can have many phases. Begin with a skill set — the skills to flip negatives into positives. Turn the skill set into a habit. Make the habit an attitude.

In the long run,
the lazy road is
often a mirage.
It starts off as a
smooth highway,
moves through
potholes on a one-
way dirt road, and
ends up on a cliff.

Mistakes
will happen.
Make amends,
learn, move
forward, don't
forget to smile
once again.

How does one identify good people? One way is to strive over a long period of time to *become* one.

If your path is difficult and diverse, realize that it cannot but sharpen your vision. Experience, shaped by a diversity of circumstances and people, helps eliminate blind spots.

As far as we humans are concerned, perfection only exists as a word. Simply, try not to confuse problems with missteps, a cliff with a solid path, sand with water, and glass with diamonds. And in a world of "spin", there are a lot of mirages.

Choose your
friends carefully.
And when they
make a misstep
and regret it,
try and help
them become a
better person.
Perhaps they will
return the favor.

Love may be demanded.
Respect may be cajoled.
These are the poor
cousins. True love and
respect are given freely.
They are earned. To
compare them to their
poor cousins, is like
comparing day to night.

Procrastination

The lazy promise ...
A reckless, unsecured bet with
time? An opulent mirage over
trapdoors. Will the drop be
insignificant or dismal?
Will the hinges be reversible or
unyielding?
What are the **names** of the
procrastinations of your life?
Weigh them carefully,
least when your hourglass runs
dry - and none know what
remains in his or her hourglass-
may not the name of any of
yours be -
soul shattering remorse.

Many people
wish they had
learnt, much
earlier in life, just
how smart their
parents were. And
just how much
they were loved.

There is so
little time to
truly enjoy
one's parents.
Don't waste
a golden
opportunity.

To have good
health, a loving
family, and
a purpose.
How blessed
can one be?

Never give up
on hope. Do not
allow darkness
to extinguish
your light. Would
you settle for a
night sky without
stars? Never.

Often people get in
life what they really,
really want. Just
make sure you really,
truly want the right
thing(s), since it may
sometimes take several
decades to get what
you want. And should
it happen that you
only end up with those
things in your life –
will you still be happy?

Want to build a better world? Why not have some fun with a group of your best friends? Experiment with starting a few sentences with the word "Imagine." Great brainstorming tool. Think boldly –where nothing is impossible. All great ideas had humble beginnings.

Ah... the
wonderful
treasures that grow
in the heart. And
empathy, patience,
perseverance
and gratitude
are but four of
the rich rivers.

A wise person uses mistakes as stepping stones on to success.

Mistakes early in life run through shallow water. The water runs deeper later in life.

The weeds of hypocrisy
can creep into an
unguarded heart – and if
hypocrisy takes powerful
root and conquers
one's heart, one is
completely and totally
ruined in the worst
possible way. Instead
plant seeds of justice,
compassion and truth
in one's heart and reap
rich harvests year after
year. Seen or unseen.

One cannot engage in heinous acts like oppressing another human with torture without scorching one's own heart and leaving a lifeless, barren desert. Likewise, one cannot engage in an act of kindness without watering the gardens of one's own heart. Every action has a reaction. Seen or unseen.

One cannot maliciously harm someone without harming oneself. Conversely, it is difficult to conscientiously help someone without helping oneself.

In the martial arts one connects with the flow of time to use an opponent's movement and energy against that person. Use the natural forces of life to propel you forward. Life is driven forward by time. Bad deeds sown may make time an enemy. Wield time as an ally in life by sowing good deeds today – don't delay! Start now!

Just because something
is simple does not
necessarily imply that
it is trivial, easy or
insignificant.
OR
Just because something
is (conceptually) simple
does not mean that it
is easy (to realize in
practice).

A good word does
not die. It inspires,
it echoes and when
it finds fertile
ground it lays
root. And then the
cycle starts anew.

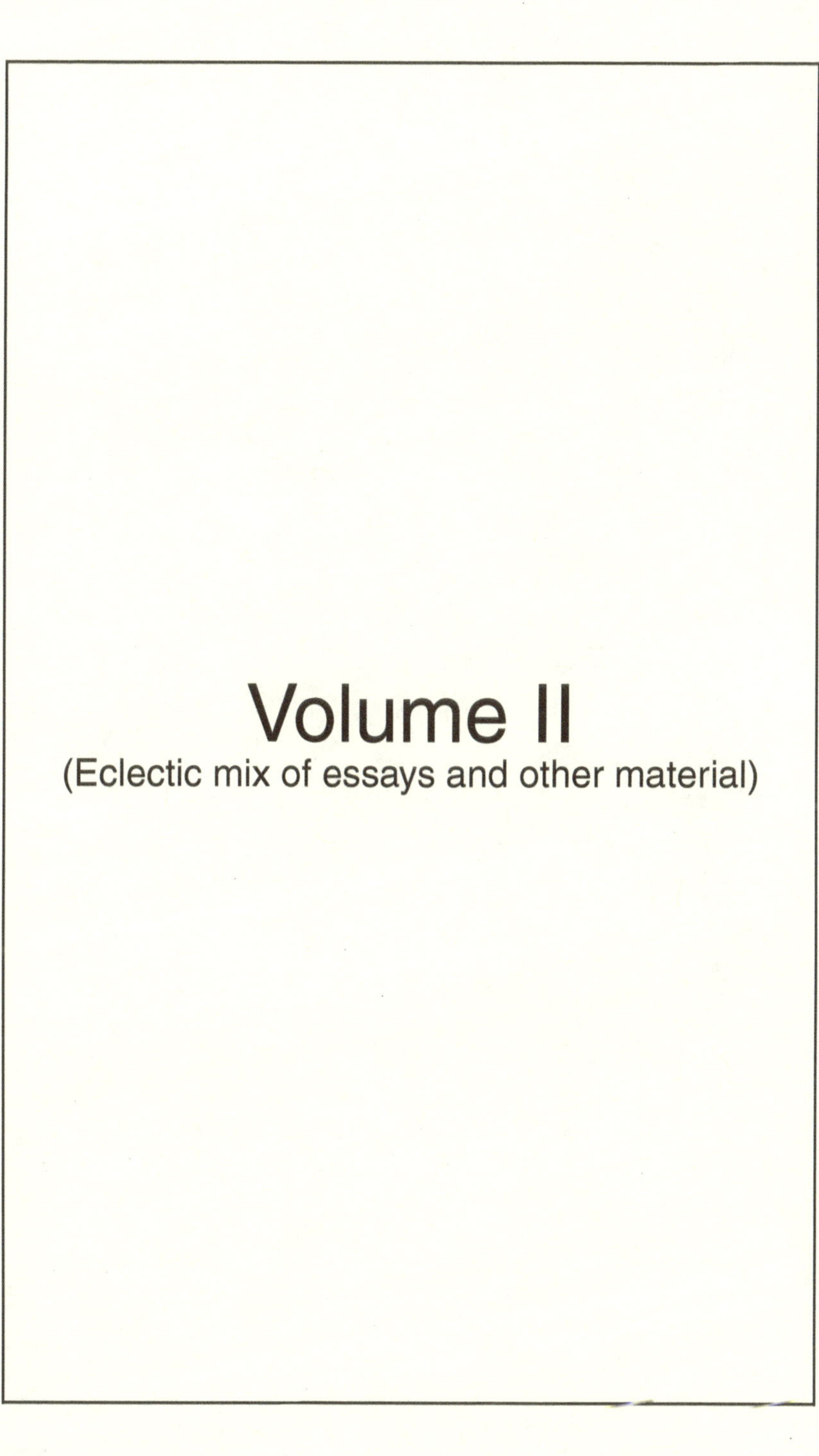

Volume II

(Eclectic mix of essays and other material)

Time

Time is a funny thing. Take a trip back in your mind, and think back to how you felt about the passage of time when you were seven years old. Can you remember what it was like riding in the back of a car for an hour. An hour seemed like six, and the only words to express it were "Are we there yet?" And what about that six months saving up for that bicycle? Six months seemed like ten years. And you couldn't wait to be as old as your older brother. Time was the last thing you thought about. And so it went.

And at some point – maybe twenty-five – you reach that in-between place where things are just about as long as they really are... You now feel comfortable with the passage of time. Yet you have a hard time imaging being sixty-five - that is if you ever think about it. More likely, sixty-five seems impossibly far away -at least as far as you are concerned. Certainly, it is going to be a very long time before **you** are sixty-five.

Time, of course, does pass and you find yourself at mid-life – that crossroads of life. At forty-five, time takes on a decidedly ambivalent hue. Where once the march of time was precise, almost mathematical, time now is marked off in rough and inexact increments. Perhaps, you find yourself searching for a spouse, or a job. As you field questions about your age, the mathematically fixed age of "forty-five" morphs into a touchy-feely "forty-something".

And yet all the while time continues to march forward inexorably. It is not long after that you find yourself enjoying retirement. At seventy, time almost seems to play tricks with your mind. Fifty years suddenly does not seem that long. As you run into a long lost college friend you think "Why, it was only yesterday that I was graduating from college."

Then, as is inevitable, you find yourself on your deathbed. Time takes on an urgency and central role it never has before. It may seem the dearest thing on the earth. "I offer half my wealth for an extra year of life," some may say. Others may wonder, "Did I spend my time well?" Where time may have once been a comma or ellipsis in one's life, it now is an emphatic exclamation mark. It simply cannot be ignored any longer.

Time is at once, precise and calculable, exotic and inscrutable. Perhaps, when all is said and done, one can only exclaim in wonder, "Time *is* a magnificent sleight of hand."

Religion - 21st Century USA Style?

If religion loses ground will this become our new religion:

Will our churches, synagogues, and mosques, in time, be replaced by the new **houses of worship** - malls? This space, a fusion of shopping and entertainment, can offer spell binding points of rapture for many. Add to it the captivating hooks of the future technologies like virtual and augmented reality that future malls might capitalize on – and an enticing mix emerges. Where will people find themselves on a Saturday, Sunday or holiday?

Will the new **clergy** be based out of that mythical land of dreams called "Hollywood?" Will "celebrities" replace priests, rabbis and imams? Will words of wisdom fall upon the rapt ears of millions of adherents from the mouth of celebrities? People who wait in line for hours, who intently parse every word, act, and gesture from their icons - icons who inhabit the land of dreams?

Who are the seers into the future? The **prophets** of these new times? The shepherds of the people? Will these be tabloids, TV pundits, talk radio, and maybe even fashion designers?

Where will we get our moral lessons for life? Our

parables, our values, our **sermons**? Will thirty minute sitcoms, concerts (song lyrics), comic books be our new sermons?

Who is **God** in this new religion? Is it the All-Mighty (Dollar)?

What about the **Day of Judgement**? Will the day(s) of Judgement be the days were we get our quarterly bank balance statements? The days where our worth as human beings is calculated and determined?

Now that the **day(s) of judgement** (see above) have been established one can easily refine the notion of **After-life**. Here are some examples of the after life. Overdrawn credit cards (e.g. living beyond one's means), plastic surgery (e.g. fooling time).

Is there a **Holy Book**? Perhaps in an era of mass customization and personalization such a book will be very personal. Maybe on the order of a self-published, do-it-yourself kind of book? It is likely to be filled with unfiltered "cut and paste" sections from **sermons** (see above). It will probably include a high tech feature to schedule periodic automatic purging/redacting of all inconvenient book passages in just one click. Warning: Procrastinators may have books with blank pages.

Proselytizing: Consigning the godlike right to author a holy book to any human would essentially allow millions of people to invent their own religion. Consider the "holy book" a murderer would write... Or a thief... Why would someone convert to another person's invented religion if they could invent their

own religion? Proselytization would cease.
Corollary: People would not have to open up their unwritten "books" to actual scrutiny , debate or examination. Without being aware of it, their "books" could contain massive inconsistencies, contradictions, and highly irregular passages.

Every religion has a **creation story** which answers the fundamental question: How did we get here? Here is a creation story: Two (very large) "Omniscient" dice rolled out our rich historical timeline.

Unfortunately, no one is really interested in the details of this creation narrative. The story of the dice did promise buzz but the topic fails to go viral. (In fact, due to an acute attention deficit virus infecting the population this topic currently only has a meager : "100 followers".)

What might be the notion of **heaven**? Sex, "Drugs" ("addicted" to TV, internet, virtual reality, etc.) and Rock & Roll?

How about **hell**?: A mirror?

(Generic Smiley)

Religion Trends? - USA

What trends might impact religion? Here are three possible trends.

1. The rise of religi-tainment: Religitainment is something that combines religion and entertainment. "If people are not coming to services why not crank up the dial on entertainment? "

2. Make religion more "customer" - centric. As the saying goes "the customer is always right." - even if the customer is wrong. Basically religion should not be demanding. At some point, demand nothing from adherents but a smile?

3. Combine religion with "feel good" pop psychology. Perhaps, run sermons like motivational speaking seminars. Do sermons really need to mention God?

What might happen to religions should such trends take root?

(Generic Smiley)

Religion by Committee?

Many people have commented on the difficulties of getting work done in an environment requiring full consensus. Ever thought about what religion might look like in such a situation? A (human created) religious book by committee may (eventually) be left with the following commandments/text (on which there is full, complete and unquestioned agreement):

First convention output:

"First there is this first sentence"
"Next there is this second sentence"
"Followed by this third sentence"...

What might happens in the second convention? Instead of focusing on content, the committee might concentrate on fine-tuning - perhaps optimization. After all, as the saying goes "time is money."

Second convention output:

Optimize the output - tear up the paper.

(Generic Smiley)

Parable of the Eyes

If one just uses one eye, or viewpoint, to see one loses the ability to perceive the richness of depth. It is no accident that we have two eyes.

Blind Egos

It has always bothered me that arrogant people ascribe success/riches overwhelmingly to themselves.

It must be asked:

Where were you born?
When were you born?
Who were your parents?
What genes were you endowed with?
And these are only the beginning of a stream of questions...

Of course, lazy people don't get ahead. While hard work and discipline are part of the story they are certainly not the *whole* story.

Own your Script

Life thrusts you many scripts ...
Some great, some ridiculous.
Several that are fun and some that are destructive.
The key is to find your very own script - from deep within yourself.
Of course, the scary (and wonderful) thing is that there are many scripts that can arise from within.
Find the one that brings out the best in you and others,
And blossom like a beautiful and exotic flower in a sun-drenched and ever-enchanting garden.
Take control.
Write your own life into happiness.

Why is Balance Important?

Why is balance important when considering things like justice, truth and compassion? What if one of these things is missing or out of balance? What might happen? If the ingredients for a recipe are out of balance the resulting final product may be sub-optimal or flawed. Spend a few minutes trying to figure out what the table below might mean.

(Potential) Issues

INPUTS			RESULT/ OUTPUT
Justice	Truth	Compassion	Issue(s)?
x	x	x	Lost
x	x	✓	Ineffective
x	✓	x	Insensitive
x	✓	✓	Chaos
✓	x	x	Revolt
✓	x	✓	Injustice
✓	✓	x	Arrogance
✓	✓	✓	Balance

How to go from a Democracy to a Dictatorship 2.0 - in twelve steps

(OR FALLING INTO THE DARK SIDE BY 12 O'CLOCK MIDNIGHT)

Are we warned and immunized?

—

(Yes, one can sometimes prevent / counteract flagrant, systemic, potential abuse of power by unmasking it.)

Just imagine for a moment that we sitting at the edge of the dictator's desk. (Forget about how we got there.) Suddenly out of the corner of our eyes we see a document. We are not sure of the title of the document. Perhaps it is "Twelve steps to shake the democratic habit", "12 second dictator", "Dictatorgate: secret memos", "Cheatsheet for dictators", or even "12 clicks to midnight." If we are to open it, it's "twelve points to dictatorship 2.0" might read as follows:

1. Carefully select a weak, dysfunctional, disliked, minority **scapegoat**. A whipping boy does wonders for the mob. (In the long run, few things transfer power to a potential dictator more readily than a mob.)

2. Do not ever miss the chance to fan the flames of **fear**. This is the most potent and explosive ingredient in the mad recipe. Institutionalize it. Set up a department of fear (just don't call it that.) Create a structural economic incentive - have the jobs of thousands of people dependent on the continuation

of fear.

Warning! There may be talk of a department of peace, in response. Do not allow this! Imagine people actually being paid to devise ideas for peace and understanding? Dangerous! Suggested dictator strategy: Ridicule any suggestions for such a department.

3. Here is another way to generate a crisis and gather more power: *create a self-reinforcing cycle of destructive energy.* You ostensibly enter the situation, most innocuously, by suggesting that you are reacting to a terrible wrong done to the nation.

And to every action, as Newton said, there is an equal and opposite reaction.

Acts invite responses. As the cycle accelerates, add fuel to the flames, by acting (or reacting) **disproportionately**, but always reminding the nation that you are simply reacting to a wrong. Of course, a cycle is two causes and effects in opposite directions, re-enforcing and feeding off each other. In other words, there may be two separate and opposite parties each claiming to be reacting to wrongs in an actual cycle. And each time one acts, the other reacts. And the initial cause(s) are quickly forgotten, as the cycle spirals madly out of control.

It is vital to cover half the cycle! Pretend it is only a direct cause and effect– definitely not a cycle. You are merely always justifiably "reacting to a wrong." Anyhow, in a period of crisis, the public will have little interest in seeing things from the other party's perspective.

Outsource any "unpleasantness" creating "plausible deniability" for the inner circle of the dictator.

On major points, be careful to shield the dictator from any *appearance* of impropriety. If he/she is not implicated in any "messiness," this will set him/her up to pardon any of his/her convicted sidekicks later on.

4. **Repeat lies.** The more often you repeat a lie the more it is taken as the truth. A well-known trick but (amazingly) still works! Bonus points: Strive to create national *myths* and *"impossible promises"* that the public believes. Myths are wonderful tools for the average person to apply as an antidote to any pesky pangs of conscience or as an excuse for just plain laziness. Occupational hazard warning: Just be careful, many dictators end up believing many of their own lies after many years.

Tip: Any myth around "security" and the incorrigible nature of the enemy (and our flawless, wonderful nature) will yield the most dividends.

Example: Total security is an exalted goal. *Total* security is attainable, and furthermore its attainment has *no important costs.* The *only* doorway to that goal is the dictator. (Of course, *total* security is probably only attainable with a descent into hell.)

"Security is mostly a superstition. It does not exist in nature, nor do the children of men as a whole experience it. Avoiding danger is no safer in the long run than outright exposure." -Helen Keller

5. **Only allow one side to be presented**. Control information. *Far more important than what is being said is what is not being said!* And as far as information about yourself goes, "transparent dictatorship" is an oxymoron. Use your "spin doctors" like pit bulls or lapdogs as needed. Bonus points: Use your control of the media to paint extreme fringe voices as the "real" voice of the opposition.

Loss of perspective. Lead the nation in collectively losing a sense of perspective. Mix/weigh inane, useless trivia as heavily as real information when launching a counter attack. (You need to look very stern, professional and serious when doing this. Do not smile/laugh.)

Framing: Only allow a situation to be viewed through a carefully selected, controlled frame for a predictable dialogue stream to result. "Focus group" everything. Airbrush the "truth", digitally manipulate the dictator's images to convey youth, vigor and honesty. Build social networks to effectively nail down the echo chambers of *group think*. Build ads around words. Learn how to make "misinformation" go viral at critical moments.

6. **Present black as white.** White as black. True patriots as traitors. Opportunists as patriots.

"Those who can make you believe absurdities can also make you commit atrocities". -Voltaire

7. Play with words. Use euphemisms. Invent new words. Own words. *Focus group core words. Corrupt words.* **Subvert language** so it begins to work for you. The awesome ROI (return on investment) on this alone would make a billionaire *blush.*

8. Make detection systems overly sensitive to the point of *pathological failure and dysfunction.* Overly sensitive systems will **identify conspiracies even when there are none.** Next, ensure there is a reward/cost asymmetry. Heavy cost to missing things. No reward for being fair. *Create moral hazards.* Do your best to subtly undermine a system of checks and balances. (e.g. Abolish any possible legal remedies for the poorest and weakest wronged groups). Skew things to your benefit.

Make an "example" of the weakest individuals. Indirectly and collectively target the weakest groups as a further "example". (Unfairly) link together people through the most tenuous of associations (e.g. Use *guilty* by association/innuendo.)

Blow up the minor imperfections of your better opponents so completely out of scale so as to *distort reality* itself. Immediately label any presentation of their real accomplishments as propaganda (and unpatriotic). *Divide and conquer.* Make your opponents fight each other. Have them do your work. Obfuscate everything: Smoke and mirrors!

The "silent majority" is, of course, silent. Exploit this.

Divide and conquer.

"First they came for the socialists, and I did not speak out – because I was not a socialist. Then they came for the trade unionists, and I did not speak out – because I was not a trade unionist. Then they came for the Jews, and I did not speak out – because I was not a Jew. Then they came for me – and there was no one left to speak for me." -Pastor Martin Niemoller. Germany. World War II era.

Use technology to your benefit. The public has no idea how fast technology is moving. Hide this from them *initially* - least they rebel in shock. There are good (and incidentally very valid) reasons for laws to lag technology. Leverage it to your advantage. If pressed, like any good illusionist, misdirect and over legislate in inappropriate ways that favor you. *Remember complexity can be your friend.* Ideally, don't produce any documents with less than 1,000 pages. *Bonus points:* **Project** the possible crimes a person *might* commit in the future. Then arrest him or her based primarily on that projection. Underline the fact that this radical but "necessary" measure proactively protects society at a time where the margin of error is so thin that failure can result in catastrophic results for the nation. However, sentence the individual *as if* he or she actually committed the crime.

9. **Make justice your own personal puppet by taking it out of balance.** Excessively shift the dial in favor of witnesses, defendants or the prosecution as and when it suits your needs. Distort the sentencing. Subvert justice by procedural delays. Experiment with selective enforcement of

laws to effectively create a two-tier system of justice.

Create a situation where a person can *accidentally* commit a crime (*without even being aware* that he or she has committed one.) Enable this by developing a code of law that is exceedingly complex, constantly changing, thousands of pages long and occasionally irrational - a lawyer's playground, a citizen's *nightmare*. The privileged rich will have the resources to find loopholes, the rest will twist in the wind - financial ruin will force them to make outrageous settlements. Enable **gag orders**: nothing can *hide/ destroy truth* (and reputations) faster. Keep the veneer of justice, but gut the inside of the building. Ideally, make the veneer as *magnificent* as possible. *Do not miss any opportunity to idolize the veneer!*

Bonus points: Exploit the specter of a threat to dramatically renegotiate the contract between the ruler and the ruled. Use emergency powers to suspend fundamental rights of the accused. *Pretend this measure is temporary.* Endeavour to create a perpetual threat yet make it appear that a solution to the threat always lurks around the corner. *Hide any suggestion that the threat has no end.*

10. Put emotions center stage. Engage in chest thumping, gut-feeling expression festivals (when useful). Embrace "pop wisdom" as needed. Few things are as effective as any pop wisdom which does not tax the brain and is devoid of serious thought and analysis. Denigrate logic as being too esoteric, costly and "ivory tower" like. **Put style ahead of substance.** The more flashy, shinning and distractive, the better. Anything to move away from

substance.

11. **Exalt entertainment.** *Every empire needs its coliseum.* Affluence is a close second choice. A great intoxicant that if done properly can quiet the tongue and still the mind.

Bonus for your image handlers (or image laundering power secret #12 on "how to dress a wolf in sheep's clothing"): *Use* charities to manage your image - *only* donate if the accompanying publicity will be picked up and disseminated to at least a million people.

12. Be arrogant, mock the humble. Silence the effective. Undermine education. Rewrite books, beginning with the *history books.*

"Who controls the past controls the future. Who controls the present controls the past." -George Orwell

Bury truth underneath several tons of bureaucracy/complexity, delaying tactics and costly lawsuits.

Are we now warned and immunized?

P.S. Obviously, this is not a real leaked "memo" or "cheatsheet." And hopefully such a 12 point "memo" will not become a real document as long as good people are vigilant.

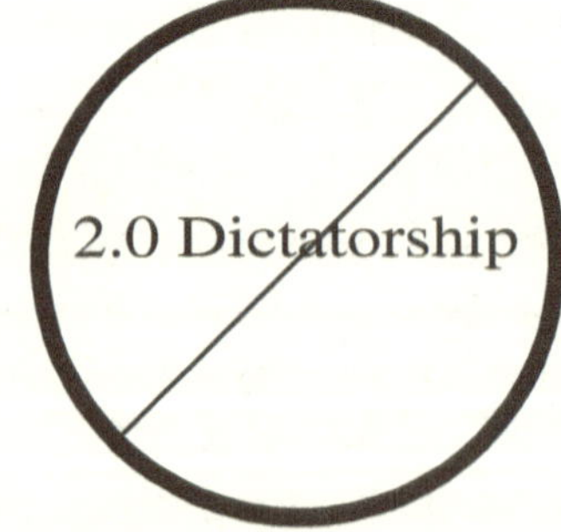

Procrastination (P)

Random equation:

$$P = \frac{(FPC + L^2 + I + IE + NR)}{(SDTGM + PO + G + HA + H + R + CV^2 + K^2 + FF + M^3)} - 0.5$$

Inputs

Increase Procrastination

FPC: Fear of failure/success, Perfectionist, Lack of confidence.
L: Laziness.
I: Ignorance. "Ignorance is bliss" gets extra points.
IE: Intoxicant Escapes. Drown problems with mind altering substances? Add several points.
NR: No Reason. Just because ... catch all variable.

Decrease Procrastination

SDTGM: Level of Self Discipline, Time/Goal management skills.
PO: Ability to postpone pleasure/tolerate hardship.
G: Level of gratefulness. It is hard to be grateful and not appreciate life - To be optimistic, happy and seek the best and most out of life.
HA: Holistic approach to life. Is life an organic inter-connected whole? Or are you continuously craving out special exceptions for entire sections of life? Do you feel the general rules of life do not apply to

numerous exceptions in your life? Do exceptions get neglected and forgotten?

H: Honesty. Specifically, how honest are you with yourself? How likely are you to lie to yourself (and believe it - at least temporarily)?

R: Responsibility. Taking responsibility for your life. Do you grab life by the horns? Are you willing to swim against the current? Or has going with the prevailing currents become a way of life?

CV: Clarity of values.

K: Knowledge.

FF: Quality of Friends/Family.

M: Level of Motivation (as determined by life changing events). Sample values: Hospital Stay = 100,000 Units. Death Bed = 100,000,000 units.

Dysfunctional Ecosystems and Peace

Dysfunctional systems can amplify minor instabilities into catastrophic chaos when there are no shock absorbers and safeguards to dampen the shock of "unexpected" bumps.

Individual people and isolated events can exert disproportionate influence into the very core of such systems. The peace of millions is thus built on a structurally flawed, unbalanced ecosystem without safeguards or shock absorbers - **systems lacking in functional models of conflict resolution, communication and power mediation.** In short, is our ecosystem a ticking time bomb of structurally dysfunctional systems?

There are many cautionary tales from history. Here are two.

Austrian Archduke Francis Ferdinand's assassination by a Serbian nationalist in Sarajevo was one of the direct causes of World War I. Through poor communication and judgment, disproportionate responses, the law of unintended consequences and a complex set of treaties between the great European powers the assassination ultimately lead to one of the worst killings in human history during the period known as World War I.

Shall humankind hurtle headlong over the proverbial cliff with brakes replaced with accelerators?

Egyptian Empire & the Hittite Empire. (The Egyptians and Hittites were the "superpowers" of the Ancient Middle East of their time.) After King Tut of Egypt died, his widow Ankhesenamun had the right to establish a new royal line of descent through remarriage. She apparently chose to marry a son of the Hittite king, instead of one of her subjects. The Hittite king Suppiluliuma saw the potential and agreed, sending his son prince Zannanza. But while traveling to Egypt the Hittite king's son was assassinated by a rival Egyptian group (possibly led by former Egyptian Grand Vizier Ay), which helped plunge the two "superpowers" into a very long running set of battles. The battle of Kadesh (1274 BCE) is one such battle which almost resulted in the death of the Egyptian pharaoh Ramesses II (and thus the loss of the Egyptian Empire).

Are "shock absorbers" really a modern invention?

Are we truly more enlightened in these matters today than during our ancient past? Careful - least we succumb to self-deception. If history is a symphony, we should be on the alert for repeating note sequences – orchestral tides portending great potential destruction. We should not fail to learn from history.

> *"While history doesn't repeat itself, it does rhyme." – Mark Twain*

Peace ...

If peace seems elusive ...
Ask: Is there justice?

If there is injustice ...
Ask: Is there truth?

If truth is difficult to find ...
Ask: Have we asked all the right questions from all angles? Of the right people from all sides (including ourselves)?

Finally Ask: Is there any courage or generosity of spirit to ease the path forward?

Peace is Not Free: The Wages of Peace

Those who seek peace, but listen only selectively, will be confronted with the anguish of an elusive mirage crumbling with each shifting breeze. Peace is not a goal, but rather a by-product. True peace, like love, cannot be forced. Its scent is more wonderful than the finest of perfumes. But she is delicate and can not survive without the mightiest of pillars feeding and sustaining her: the truly awe inspiring pillars of truth, justice and compassion.

If the price of war is so high, why are we so stingy in paying the wages of peace?

Generosity – The Mirror

Personally, I believe it is not possible to give without receiving. Generosity of any kind, boomerangs in odd and unexpected ways. In a path that is sometimes short or one that winds exceedingly long. Each act of generosity resonates like a different note in an orchestra. As does it's counterpart: stinginess.

Our delays in finding cures for things like cancer, or heart disease is a reflection of this law.

The brilliant researcher that would smite the scourge of cancer is born to a homeless family in a poor, forgotten nation. She dies from a simple disease. Her death could have been prevented by a vaccine that could cost a few pennies.

But we had once asked what could just one person do, with just a few pennies to contribute?

Someone who would revolutionize heart disease has a promising beginning but is born in a less promising nation. His family knew he was smart but they could not afford to enroll him in school when he was young. He dies a brilliant mind, his promise unfulfilled, sweeping the streets to feed his own family when he grows older.

But we had asked why should we care what happens half a world away?

Who does our stinginess hurt but ourselves?

Oh, but what could be? Oh what could be!

Prisoners of War (POWs)

During war, when one side has suffered losses there is sometimes an impulse to seek retribution. When some soldiers see their friends have been killed, they may decide to exact retribution on the POWs of the other side. War accounts are not without stories of surrendering troops being killed.

Why not treat POWs and surrendering troops extremely well instead? Is this really counter intuitive?

Which approach do you think will lead to fewer future casualties? Which approach will prolong a war? Does transgression of rules by one side not invite a similar response from the other side?

The Paradox of Spending on Weapons (in the Modern Era) and Accidental Catastrophe.

Throughout history the smart money has bet on the importance of investing in weapons in order to defend oneself. But today there is a possible game changer: *extraordinary (and accelerating) advances in technology.* Furthermore, the advances in technological offense and defense capabilities may not be concurrent – potentially creating massive instability.

For example, if there is an **accident** involving nuclear weapons the time to resolve and rectify the situation is frighteningly low. There is a very short interval for a nuclear power to decide on a response if it perceives the other side has launched nuclear missiles. The perception may be incorrect, or the launch may have been accidental. The clock still ticks on a very small window. The frightening thing is that technological advances are threatening to dramatically contract this already tiny window. The potential devastation from miscalculations is unimaginable.

By pouring money into arms there is a danger of inadvertently adding fuel to fire if that money results in dramatic technology leaps that, for example, whittle the response time down to an impossibly difficult to manage tiny time slot. This creates a potentially highly unstable situation.

And today's technology has gone far beyond just nuclear missiles. Technology advances promise many new (including yet unimagined) non-nuclear weapons of mass destruction. Technology advances promise many new (including yet unimagined) non-missile delivery mechanisms. Furthermore, each of these individual technologies is simultaneously experiencing its own exponential curve of technological advance.

Should not defense spending became smarter? To truly defend ourselves, should that spending not become more diverse? Spending that in addition also includes non-technology and imaginative solutions. Spending on peace. Spending to solve root problems. Build bridges. Raise levels of education. Unite economies.

Today, everyday we are waking up and thanking ourselves that an accident has not happened and/or that we have not lost control of our own technology.

Deluge of Power

The low have laid siege to the dam of power - blind puppets to their desires. Centuries of relentless attacks are on the verge of humbling the ancient dam. Once the wise sought power, but were checked by a healthy fear of it. Once the majestic dam vigorously guarded its treasure only yielding small streams.

But gone is the vigor and as the old dam teeters, madness has trumped reason. Moths quicken their orbits towards that alluring flame that beckons. Wise men and fools battle for the last ramparts of might before the highest cliffs. Seemingly locked together in a relentless wheel hurtling in a death spiral into the night.

Now will weak men taste the paradox of the absolute power they so sought? Or will man finally look inside himself, lift himself, and take that difficult flight into the stars?

Volume III
(Short Story Fiction)

The Man, the Mosquito and the Hut

"Shall I tell you the story of the man and the mosquito?" the storyteller asked.

"Yes", the villagers chimed enthusiastically.

"Well there was once a large man who awoke bitten by a tiny mosquito. Being rightly aggrieved he searched for his axe to squash the pesky bugger. 'Ah! There!' The man grunted as he wielded his axe directly at the mosquito. Missed! He heard a loud crunch of wood in the dark.

He adjusted himself a little better, and rubbed his eyes. The mosquito almost seemed to dance its way to the wall on his left. The man felt a slight twang of irritation. He squinted his eyes, and swung his axe against the insect. He just missed, but he thought he had clipped part of the mosquito's wing. He swung again - this time a little faster, harder. He felt a thud, the wall beam cracked. But where was that mosquito? He must have got it.

He felt a little uncertain, and was still half-asleep. But he was tired, and so he more of less rolled back into his bed. A few moments later, he heard the telltale buzz of his mosquito. He was getting really annoyed.

He leaped out his bed furiously swinging his axe back and forth. The man marveled at how quickly he smashed his axe against the hut walls. There was no way for the mosquito to escape now. His axe was a whirl of action against the backdrop of his hut. That must have done it. 'The mosquito is certainly no more' he declared most emphatically after a few minutes of action.

He barely finished before, out of the corner of his eye, he saw the walls begin to collapse around him. He rushed out of his hut. Just in time, before the roof of his hut fell in."

At this point the storyteller was interrupted.

"All this just for a mosquito? I also heard that story. In fact, it was not a mosquito, but a mosquito and a bat.", another villager piped in.

"Both of you are wrong. It was not a mosquito or just a bat. It was a three big bloodthirsty vampire bats." a second villager jumped in.

The storyteller stopped. "...it was a mosquito." The storyteller continued ...

"As the man slowly began to realize what had just happened, he thought it wise to sit down. As he looked into his large hands, he wondered just how he was going to phrase the events that transpired when his diminutive, yet so articulate wife, returned to their hut later that day. 'Maybe I just should have swatted the mosquito with my hands', the big man thought ruefully."

A Most Unnatural Day

The sights and sounds of the massive war were everywhere. The sound of explosions and gunshots never seemed to cease. This battle was in full earnest. A bomb exploded in the distance, to my left, releasing a strange purple gas.

I lifted my gun, and saw the enemy in my sights. He had a funny scar over his right eye. My finger tightened on the trigger. Then without explanation a strange thing happened. Time suddenly seemed to slow down. A pulsating light suddenly came out of nowhere and I heard a voice that startled me.

A translucent older woman eerily floated just above me and then spoke: "That is my son you are about to kill!" I was too surprised to speak and just mumbled, reflexively wondering if she possessed any "supernatural" powers to destroy me in her rage. I was surprised and shocked by my thoughts. "Don't worry; I am not going to harm you. Instead let me tell you about my son", the woman said gently.

How was this even possible? Was I hallucinating? Was I going insane? My thoughts moved at a hundred miles per hour.

She continued, "You know, my son and you are about the same age. If fate had been just a little different, perhaps you would have been fast friends. I know that you volunteered in soup kitchens feeding the poor." I wondered how she could have known that. "My son volunteered digging drinking wells for the poor. That is where he injured his right eyebrow. He was very hesitant to join this war, in the beginning. I wish I had still been alive to talk to him about those feelings."

As my thoughts turned away from the woman, I remembered my early misgivings too, but I was doing this for my own sons I thought. But I was drawn back to the woman.

The woman nodded "Yes, that is what my son also thought - that he was doing it for his daughters," she said.

I lowered my gun. The man who was my sights now turned his gun at me. I froze.

Suddenly, a bewildered look came on his face, and he violently turned the gun away from me as it fired. Then he and I both sat in a trance, both of us uncertain about what was still real and what had just happened.

I turned my gun completely away from him and fired into the air. I hoped our leaders had fewer innocent people than evil people killed today. Surely there was a better way to target the bad guys. Surely their entire alliance wasn't evil? Was this really the best way to resolve our issues? Maybe both sides should have questioned our leaders more closely before letting it come to this. "Only an ounce of questions to stop the pound of war." My mind was acting strangely mixing metaphors. I had an strangely uncomfortable feeling in the pit of my stomach.

The floodgates of war once opened are not easily closed. The battle would continue. But we both deliberately walked to opposite ends of the battle.

I did wonder what my mom told the man with the scar about me this fateful day.

Would we both survive the day? Or would we meet at a better, fairer world? How many millions would die in war that few wanted any more? I was feeling quite ill by now.

Then I shuddered with a thought - perhaps I was dead but just did not know it yet. Reflexively, I immediately reached over to try to pinch myself awake. Hopefully, it would work ...

"If you had only known the man you were trying to kill, you would have risked your life, to save his."
Harry Pope, World War II, Pacific 1944 - Occupied Japan, 1950

"They make a desert and call it peace."

Tacitus, on Roman imperialism

On Writing a Story... (Practicality and Virtue)

How meaningful is it too say that one believes in mercy? Unless confronted, no tested, in belief of that virtue? Is merely saying that mercy is an excellent quality like announcing that fish swim in water?

Now consider the captain in a frantic, continuously shifting, pitched battle, in a desperate struggle for survival, with a terrible decision to make. One of his privates says kill the captive. Another says make him a prisoner of war (POW).

Is one decision generally better than the other is? What decision makes more sense rationally, intellectually? Which path should one take? The currents are terrifyingly strong.

Of course, either path can be intellectually defended. In life, is a step to the right better than a step to the left? A step to the right will have some benefits and some drawbacks as will a step to the left. As in a game of chess, one step alone dissolves before the twisting, ever-escalating, crescendo of moves life throws at one - a reaction by life almost surprisingly filled with noise and intelligence.

Shall we join the captain?

The captain knew that the position of his troops was desperate. A POW would slow them down, incapacitating them in critical life and death situations. The situation was so fragile, a false move might even allow the POW to sabotage them at a critical moment. Was the POW bobby trapped? Not enough time to check. The easiest, most logical step just might be to shoot him now.

Reinforcements were said to be on the way. But if he shot the captive, they were still deep in enemy territory. The shooting of a POW would enrage the enemy. They would double their resources to hunt down his team. Instead of losing a few men, he might lose all his men to the new, insatiable rage of the enemy. And then again, he just might also lose a part of himself.

Was he taking too much time to decide? He was so hyper alert, he could almost feel the sands shifting and reshaping through the hourglass of time.

He wondered how it was interesting in life that decisions could seem so obvious, a path so alluring in the moment, but how in the end everything could be so neutral. Perhaps everything, that is, but his nature.

The captain considered all his options. He made his decision. A snapshot of one's nature - stripped to its core.

And then the dice of life rolled forward inexorably... Thus were the lives of men shaped and indelibly written- etched in a manner at once, sublime and wretched, yet completely undeniable. A recording scroll extended through time. ***Not neutral, but facing oneself.***

A Mother's Love

The young officer was a tall, confident and handsome man. It was surprising he was here. He was a bright and articulate man - a scion of a powerful family and a product of the best schools. He could have written his own ticket anywhere. His tribe dominated the fulcrum of power for the human race. Yet when called, he had come here. Had come here because, the leaders had said the balance of peace depended on it. His beautiful, young wife may have understood his decision intellectually, but it did not make it less difficult. She tried to be strong, to trust the right people, to do her part. If nothing else, she had to be strong for her children.

It had been difficult for the officer too. Was he or was his wife carrying the greater burden? But he had always been taught to do the right thing. His courage was not going to fail him now.

All that now that seemed so long ago. The officer sat down. Thick smoke enveloped him. The place was a smothering ruin with wreckage strung everywhere. One could hear gunfire in the distance.

The officer replayed the argument he had had yesterday with private Darv. Darv was a hothead, a loud, arrogant private. And one with very few scruples. To him the ends justified the means. There was always only one side to an argument - Darv's side. The officer detested Darv.

One of the officer's columns had been attacked yesterday. "Burn the whole worthless village to the ground," said Darv. "These people are not people they are animals! Every one of them is guilty." The group was tired. It had gone 36 hours without sleep and suffered heavy casualties. "Darv, we are not murderers. We are here to help build a better life for these people, not kill innocent people," said the officer. But Darv persisted, the men were very angry and had blood in their eyes. "Do you think these animals cared when they killed our former company commander? Or our sergeant last week? Or even the poor guy who was on foot patrol yesterday? How many more of your men will these 'values' cost us?" Darv bordered on insubordination. For the first time a flash of anger crossed the officer's normally calm eyes. "Private! If we lose the hearts of these people the resulting casualties will dwarf those we now have."

The officer flashed back to the present. He was leading a small experimental integrated tactical ground and airborne reconnaissance unit. They were on their way back to the base when they had surprised a few rebels. In fact the two groups had surprised each other, near a location uncomfortably close to a crowded civilian area. Fortunately, the officer had the better tactical position when he noticed the guns, and his unit had immediately gone into cover.

"Enemy five o'clock", The officer barked diving for cover. Almost immediately, he noticed two men peel away from the small enemy group and head for the crowds. "Do not fire into the civilians. Target the rebel group directly. Now!" The officer yelled. He quickly glanced at Darv and noticed him curl his lips and swing the gun back to the rebel group. At just about this time, a rebel briefly jumped into view. "Idiot!" thought Darv. He coolly aimed and fired. The target dropped out of sight. It looked like a brief firefight. The officer's well armed, tactically positioned men seemed to quickly disperse the surprised rebels.

...

The tall, handsome dark man in the long flowing white robes had never had any interest in fighting. After completing the final year of his religious studies, he hoped to open a shelter for orphaned children in a poor part of town. They were so desperate. He had been so blessed. It was the least he could do.

Now it all seemed so far away. In retrospect, perhaps the nightmare had begun on that day - the day he had visited his teacher at their house of worship. Suddenly, without much warning, a bomb had hit the structure's roof, shattering the calm that normally envelopes all houses of worship. The religious leader was dead instantly, along with a number of others. He himself however had miraculously escaped – without a scratch on him, but his life had been shaken to the core. His religious leader had been wise, a kind, and gentle soul. In the chaos and vacuum that followed, the poor and downtrodden had lost their best protector.

In the days that followed, he changed. He had never carried a gun before. But when he had been powerless to protect a woman from been raped, he realized that the local thugs were launching a reign of terror upon his neighborhood. Soon there were people being strung up, and numerous random bombings –the brunt of which was borne by the poorest and weakest segments of society.

Reluctantly, he started carrying a gun. By himself, he could do nothing to improve the situation, so he joined a rebel group. 'Criminal' group was more like it, the new rebel recruit quickly learnt. Things like petty theft, extortion. But he was going to change that. He cared about the people. He knew he needed to find out where the rebels and his people stood. He then recruited a few of his friends from his studies that he knew could help him take over the local corrupt warlord's turf. He became a hidden rebel leader within the warlord's own group with the aim to improve things. He was going to leave a better world to his children.

He and his friends trained hard. The "coup" would take place in a few days. The criminals would end their reign of darkness in his neighborhood. It was very risky of course. But the rebel leader and his friends were not about to simply roll over without trying. Truth, justice and compassion would soon no longer continue take a back seat in his neighborhood. The tyrant warlord's reign of terror would soon end. One location with one or two villages, not much, perhaps, but it was his world.

...

Today, the rebel leader decided to visit the local warlord's place. But as he approached a small group was leaving. They were taking a break and asked him to join them. Some were the rebel leader's friends. Two others, both outfitted with matching sunglasses, were new, and strutted with a odd mixture of ignorance and arrogance - he did not really know them. This motley group decided to stop by the marketplace.

As they rounded the corner galloping on their horses, the group saw a bunch of soldiers dive behind a wall. "Soldiers!" someone yelled. The scene collapsed on the rebel side in a mayhem of confusion as arms and legs flew in all directions in a frantic struggle for the what little there was for cover.

The rebel leader saw the two men with sunglasses break from his group and head into the crowd. He was not going to allow them put women and children in danger. He made a quick decision. The rebel leader stood up very briefly so that he could yell and stop them firing from the crowd. But it was not quick enough. He took a direct hit himself.

As the rebel leader's eyes turned, his lips parted in surprise. He let out a grasp. Then he appeared to say something, in horror, in what almost seemed to be a foreign tongue. His eyes seemed glazed as he hit the ground.

...

The officer surveyed the scene. Some of the rebels had fled. Some had been killed. The officer, was glad that despite his conversation with Darv earlier, he could note that his unit had fought honorably. The officer had lost too many friends, to dishonor them in death by threading on the best ideals of his nation. He knew the only way to win the war was to genuinely, convince his surviving enemies that they shared common values and thus willingly convert an former enemy to a friend.

That Darv was an idiot. He just did not understand. It was impatient, lazy people like Darv that had made the army go from a winning army to a losing one. But when fear gripped men, people like Darv became more difficult to check, and people like the officer did not find the receptive ear they had once so readily found. People like the officer were honored, but he worried about how much actual power people like him had lost.

The officer was broken from his thoughts, as one of his men accidently knocked over one of bodies of the rebels. His men were doing a quick, cursory search for booby traps, intelligence. Routine military stuff –although admittedly some of the stuff was hard to catch on the fly. The man whose body had been jarred to the side looked like their leader. As the body rolled it exposed an object, lying on the man's chest just barely exposed over in a large pool of blood. The officer saw it lazily from the corner of his eyes.

He then froze instantly.

His eyes clouded in utter confusion. Involuntarily, his body convulsed in horror. As he froze in time, he did not hear his men scatter in disarray as they yelled "incoming" and dove for cover. Two men with matching shades shot from the crowd of civilians.

All the officer saw was the unattended object on the

dead enemy leader as the world began to collapse around him. The officer had taken a fatal hit. His eyes covered the fallen body even as his own life began to slip away from him. In his last passing breath, his eyes, now cold, struggled searching for Darv.

"Fools!" thought Darv as he managed to slip in behind the controls of the high tech cockpit just as he saw several of his companions fall. The powerful armored machine lifted into the sky. His eyes were red and cold – filled with hatred. The blood pounded in his head in rhythm as he methodically a pressed button after button firing directly into the crowded marketplace. Suddenly he slumped as a stray bullet miraculously cut him down. The horizon then filled in slow motion, with the flaming mass barreling into a terrible death dive.

Soon after the massacre at the marketplace, locals were outraged. Many innocent women and children had been killed. Rebel recruitment skyrocketed that day. The next month looked like it was going to be the bloodiest one on record.

...

Reporters Judy Tanaka and Kumiko Johansson approached the scene in silence. A rag here, a memory there, fluttered solemnly as a mild, gentle breeze descended on them. They took care to begin properly surveying and recording items from the recent battle scene.

A number of things at the "scene" had struck Judy After several exhaustive queries, pulling some strings, and several hours in deep research, she had answered some nagging questions. Now the results lay before her.

"So you are saying that the officer and the rebel leader both had the same lockets around their necks?" said Kumiko. "Yes," said Judy. "I was surprised since the officer is one of the finest soldiers." "But imagine my shock, when upon closer inspection, I noticed the 'lockets' were actually two halves of one locket that matched exactly.

The locket seems to have belonged to their mother Mary. Mary was twice married. Her first husband died young in a vehicle crash back home. The officer is their son. Mary then married someone from here. The rebel leader is the son from that marriage. The rebel's father died shortly after his birth. Mary herself passed away unexpectedly many years ago. All this happened before the war started - quite a series of unfortunate family tragedies.

I heard that when the officer and rebel were little they were inseparable (step) brothers. Their mother surrounded them with abundant, unconditional love. She taught them good morals. They felt secure and at peace. Suddenly, an accident left them without parents.

Since they were so little when their parents passed

on, they had to depend on each other. They frequently defended each other when people picked on them because they were so different. But people recalled that if the two were ever backed into the wall by the bigger bullies they would still remain at each other's side.

They stuck together until the relatives from the different families claimed them and they ended up in different countries, through a succession of distant relatives. They lost track of each other after they were (incorrectly) told that the other one had died. But they never forgot about each other." "I didn't know," Kumiko said.

"I cannot even fathom what the officer thought when he saw the locket on the rebel leader's heart," Judy replied.

"I was told that there was also a beautiful inscription on the locket. What did it say?" said Kumiko. Judy looked at her for a long moment, and then replied, 'The only thing that can save our world is love. "

Time Court

A billionaire lay on his deathbed. He suddenly realized how much of his life he had wasted. What exactly had he accomplished with his life?

His thoughts bounced wildly in his head at a thousand miles an hour:

Him: I will offer a billion dollars for an extra month to live!

Court Official #1: You could have had it for much less before.

Him: I offer two billion.

Court Official #2: Why should you get more time? You spent total three years of your life solidly watching TV. Are you worthy of the *gift* of time?

Him: ... Is that fair?

Court Official #1: As you used to say in life. "Past performance is actually a good indicator of future performance."

Him: Did I?

Court Official #1: Yes. Just before you laid off a number of people.

Court Official #2:
2 years protecting your wealth.
4 year worrying about your wealth.
1.5 years arguing with your wife.
1 year buying toys for yourself.

Court Official #1 [Quietly]: One year buying toys? It took 6 years to get enough money to be able to buy those toys!

Court Official #2:
25 years in sleep.
4 years eating.
3 years traveling.
... And there is much more on this balance sheet.

Him: Well if you aggregate over a lifetime ...

Court Official #3: Did you not have a long life? How long does it take to say a kind word? To smile? To plant a tree? To help someone step out of a ditch?

Court Official #2: Are you saying you did not have a long life?

Him: I ...

Court Official #1: And as far as effort goes, the effort involved diminishes rapidly when something becomes a habit.

Him: This is not going well is it?

[Voices start to fade ...]

Him: Is someone dimming the lights?

Offers

If we find any offers or products that we think our book readers might be interested in, we will post them at the book website. Please do check out:

www.StopRestAndThink.com
www.DesertWellNetwork.com

(For example we are thinking of putting a list of book discussion questions for use in a book club or classroom situation.)

Notes

www.ingramcontent.com/pod-product-compliance
Lightning Source LLC
LaVergne TN
LVHW091008080826
845145LV00003B/1182

9781592360031